PRESSURE COOKER COOKBOOK

Amazingly Delicious Plant-based Recipes for Healthy Meals

(Fast, Savory and Good for Health Recipes)

Logan Poff

Published by Sharon Lohan

© Logan Poff

All Rights Reserved

Pressure Cooker Cookbook: Amazingly Delicious Plant-based Recipes for Healthy Meals (Fast, Savory and Good for Health Recipes)

ISBN 978-1-990334-24-5

All rights reserved. No part of this guide may be reproduced in any form without permission in writing from the publisher except in the case of brief quotations embodied in critical articles or reviews.

Legal & Disclaimer

The information contained in this book is not designed to replace or take the place of any form of medicine or professional medical advice. The information in this book has been provided for educational and entertainment purposes only.

The information contained in this book has been compiled from sources deemed reliable, and it is accurate to the best of the Author's knowledge; however, the Author cannot guarantee its accuracy and validity and cannot be held liable for any errors or omissions. Changes are periodically made to this book. You must consult your doctor or get professional medical advice before using any of the suggested remedies, techniques, or information in this book.

Table of contents

Part 1 1

Introduction 2

Fancy Chocolate Fondue 4

Hummus 5

Cherry Jam 7

Chili Sauce 9

Deviled Eggs 11

Bone Broth 13

Pressure Corn 15

Hearty Cauliflower Soup 17

Creamy Mushroom Soup 19

Creamy Sweet Potato Soup 21

Parmesan Risotto 23

Bell peppers Salad 26

Asparagus Risotto 28

Cheese Burger Pasta 30

Sausages Sandwiches 32

Chicken Spring Rice Casserole 34

Zuppa Tuscana 36

Onion Soup 38

Black Eyed Sausage Soup 41

Garbanzo Macaroni Minestrone 44

Tuna Spaghetti 47

Green Beans Sauté 49

Sesame Chicken Wings 51

Prosciutto Chicken 53

Spicy Pressure Bows 56

Chicken Butter 58

Pulled Apple Chicken 60

Mustard Chicken Curry 62

Spaghetti Meatballs 64

Apple Pork Roast 66

Cottage Pie 68

Juicy Chicken Breasts 71

Moroccan Lamb and Prunes Tajine	73
Turkey Beans Chili	75
Italian Chicken Marinara	77
Honey Chicken	79
Ranch Chicken	81
Bell Chicken Pasta	83
Chili Onion Chicken Pasta	85
Corny Chicken Pasta	88
Loaded Chicken Soup	90
Chipotle Brisket	92
Shredded Beef Burgers	94
Greek Style Stew	96
Brisket Pot	98
Flat Brisket with Gravy	100
Wine Pears	102
Chocolate Cake	103
Apple Cake	106
Christmas Pudding	108

Part 2 111

Introduction 112

Breakfast Recipes 113

1. Pressure Cooker Quinoa 113

2. Apple Cinnamon Steel Cut Oats 115

3. Carrot Cake Oatmeal 117

4. Pumpkin Oats With Pecan Pie Granola 119

5. Pressure Cooker Cinnamon Bread Pudding With Caramel Pecan Sauce 121

6. Blueberry Lemon Oats 124

7. Tapioca Pudding 126

8. Breakfast Rice pudding 128

9. Peaches And Creamy Oats 130

Soup Recipes 131

10. Sweet Potato Cheese soup 131

11. Butternut Squash Soup With Chicken 134

12. Pressure Cooker Mushroom Stock 137

13. Pressure Cooker Chicken, And Chorizo Soup 138

14. Creamy Wild Rice And Chicken Soup 140

15. Tomato Parmesan soup 142

16. Pressure Cooker Garden minestrone soup.......................... 144

17. Chicken Noodle Soup.. 146

18. Chicken Stock.. 148

19. Pressure Cooker Portobello Mushroom And Barley Soup
.... 150

Main Dishes.. 152

20. Spinach And Whole-Wheat Fusilli.. 152

21. Pressure Cooker Rice And Lentil Pilaf..................................... 154

22. Pressure Cooker Pulled BBQ Beef Sandwiches.................. 156

23. Chicken Pumpkin Corn Chowder... 157

24. Pressure Cooker Spicy Honey Chicken 159

25. Chicken Enchilada Pasta 161

26. Almond Saffron Rice Pilaf... 163

27. Minestrone Soup With Basil Pesto.. 165

28. French Dip Sandwiches.. 167

29. Grains And Kale Salad 168

30. Pressure Cooker Smothered burritos 170

Side Dishes 171

31. Pressure Cooker Sun dried herbed tomato polenta 171

32. Baked Beans 173

33. Green Rice 176

34. Rosemary Garlic Potatoes 177

35. Thai Quinoa Salad 178

36. Pork Sirloin Tip roast 181

37. Pressure Cooker Black Bean Rice Salad 183

38. Pressure Cooker Black Beans 185

Conclusion 186

Part 1

Introduction

Pressure cookers with food are like the godmother fairy with Cinderella, it turns several plain ingredients into a scrumptious good looking meal!

Pressure cookers are one of those incredible kitchen utensils that came to save our busy lives and save us a lot of time by having cozy homemade meals that can be prepared in minutes!

It is not a rocket science or a utensil that will need a lot of your attention to use it which makes perfect and a necessity in every kitchen counter! Who doesn't want to put a couple of ingredients in a pot then let them cook for few minutes to turn out into an incredible meal that will leave you moaning and thanking God for it?!!

Not to mention that anyone can use it, you don't have to be a chef or someone who cooks every day! Anyone can use it and benefit from it for it is the time to say goodbye to those stoves and pots that trap you in the kitchen most of the day and when you finally finish cooking in them you end up with loads of dishes to wash!

If you already have a pressure cooker, good for you! If you don't have it; you better run to the store right now or order it online for you are missing a lot and if you take a look at the recipes below in this book, you will see what I am talking about! 50 delicious sweet, sour, salty and spicy recipes that will blow your mind and you can prepare them with simple ingredients by following some very simple steps!

Once you try one of them, you will know how food can be scrumptious and more delicious when it is cooked in a pressure cooker because unlike regular pots and oven, it traps the flavors that try to escape from it with the steam inside of it and force it to go back to the food which make it more delicious and melts in the mouth!

So get that apron on to show and impress everybody even you with your cooking skills and delicious food!

Fancy Chocolate Fondue

(Prep Time: 12 min | Cooking Time: 5 min | Servings 2)

Ingredients:

- 3.5 ounces of half and half
- 3.5 ounces of bittersweet chocolate, roughly chopped
- 1 teaspoon of sugar

Directions:

1. Pour 1 cup of water in a pressure cooker and lower in it a steamer rack.

2. Combine all the ingredients in a container or ramekin then place it on the steamer rack.

3. Put on the lid and bring the pot to pressure then cook it for 1 min on high pressure.

4. Once the time is up, use the natural method to release the pressure.

5. Serve your chocolate fondue and enjoy.

Hummus

(Prep Time: 15 min | Cooking Time: 15 min | Servings 4)

Ingredients:

- 1 cup of chickpeas, soaked for an overnight
- 6 cups of water
- The juice of 1 lemon
- 2 tablespoons of tahini
- 2 tablespoons of parsley, finely chopped

- 1 tablespoon of olive oil
- ½ teaspoon of paprika
- ¼ teaspoon of cumin
- 2 cloves of garlic, minced
- Black pepper
- Salt

Directions:

1. Combine the chickpeas with a pinch of salt and water in a pressure cooker then put on the lid and cook it for 15 min on high pressure.

2. Once the time is up, use the natural method to release the pressure.

3. Drain the chickpeas and transfer them to a food processor with the tahini, cumin, lemon juice and garlic, paprika, parsley, a pinch of salt and pepper then blend them smooth.

4. Serve your hummus and enjoy.

Cherry Jam

(Prep Time: 15 min | Cooking Time: 10 min | Servings 6)

Ingredients:

- 17.5 ounces of sweet cherries
- 8.5 ounces of preserving sugar
- 2 fresh sprigs of rosemary leaves
- The juice of ½ lemon
- The zest of ½ lemon, grated

Directions:

1. Combine the lemon juice and zest with rosemary and cherries in a food processor and blend them smooth.

2. Pour the mix into a heavy saucepan with the sugar then bring them to a rolling boil for 3 min while stirring all the time.

3. Transfer the jam to canning jars and seal them.

4. Pour 1 cup of water in the bottom of a pressure cooker and lower a steaming rack in it then place the jars on it.

5. Put on the lid and cook them for 3 min on high pressure then use the quick method to release the pressure.

6. Store your jars in a dark area and serve it whenever you desire.

Chili Sauce

(Prep Time: 15 min | Cooking Time: 8 min | Servings 12)

Ingredients:

- 6 pounds of tomato, roughly chopped
- 3 yellow onions, finely chopped

- 3 tablespoons of olive oil
- 2 tablespoons of chili peppers, minced
- 6 cloves of garlic, peeled
- 1 sprig of fresh thyme
- 1 teaspoon of dry basil
- 1 teaspoon of cumin
- 1 teaspoon of Salt

Directions:

1. Combine all the ingredients in a pressure cooker then put on the lid and cook them for 8 min on high pressure.

2. Once the time is up, use the natural method to release the pressure then allow the sauce to cool down slightly.

3. Transfer the sauce to a food processor and blend it smooth then store it or use it right away and enjoy.

Deviled Eggs

(Prep Time: 15 min | Cooking Time: 7 min | Servings 24)

Ingredients:

- 12 eggs
- ¼ cup of sour cream
- 2 tablespoons of butter, melted
- 1 tablespoon of Dijon mustard
- 2 teaspoon of lime juice
- Black pepper
- Salt

Directions:

1. Pour 1 cup of water in a pressure cooker and lower in it the steamer basket then place the eggs in it.

2. Put on the lid and cook the eggs for 7 min on high pressure.

3. Once the time is up, use the natural method to release the pressure.

4. Peel the eggs and cut them in half.

5. Spoon the egg yolk into a separate bowl then set the cooked egg white aside.

6. Add the mustard with lime juice, sour cream, a pinch of salt and pepper to the egg yolks then beat them with a hand mixer until they become creamy.

7. Spoon the mix into a piping bag and pipe it into the egg white shells then serve them and enjoy.

Bone Broth

(Prep Time: 15 min | Cooking Time: 2 h 45 min | Servings 6)

Ingredients:

- 3 pounds of beef/lamb/chicken bones
- 1 handful of peppercorns
- 1 tablespoon of apple cider vinegar
- 1 bay leaf
- Water
- Black pepper

Directions:

1. Preheat the oven on 365 F.

2. Place the bones in a roasting pan and roast them for 45 min while turning them every once in a while.

3. Once the time is up, transfer the bones to a pressure cooker with the remaining ingredients and cover them with water.

4. Put on the lid and cook them for 2 h on low pressure.

5. Once the time is up, strain the broth then store it or serve it and enjoy.

Pressure Corn

(Prep Time: 10 min | Cooking Time: 2 min | Servings 8)

Ingredients:

- 8 ears of corn

Directions:

1. Pour 2 cups of water in the bottom of a pressure cooker then lower into a steamer rack.

2. Place the ears of corn on the rack then put on the lid and cook them for 2 min on high pressure.

3. Once the time is up, use the natural method to release the pressure.

4. Serve you corn with some butter and enjoy.

Hearty Cauliflower Soup

(Prep Time: 15 min | Cooking Time: 12 min | Servings 4)

Ingredients:

- 1 pound of cauliflower florets
- 1 yellow onion, finely chopped
- 1 stalk of celery, finely chopped
- 5 ounces of smoked cheddar cheese
- 4 cups of chicken stock

- ¾ cup of half and half cream
- 2 egg yolks, beaten
- 2 tablespoons of vegetable oil
- 1 clove of garlic, minced
- Black pepper
- Salt

Directions:

1. Press the sauté button on the pressure cooker then sauté in it the onion with celery and garlic for 5 min.

2. Stir in the cauliflower with stock, a pinch of salt and pepper then put on the lid and cook them for 8 min on high pressure.

3. Once the time is up, use the natural method to release the pressure.

4. Whisk the cream with egg yolks then add 1 cup of broth from the pot and whisk them until they become smooth.

5. Transfer the mix into the pot with the cheese and stir them.

6. Blend the soup smooth with an Immersion blender then serve it warm and enjoy.

Creamy Mushroom Soup

(Prep Time: 15 min | Cooking Time: 20 min | Servings 4)

Ingredients:

- 1 ½ pounds of mushroom, sliced
- 2 red potatoes, diced
- 1 red onion, finely chopped
- 1 stalk of celery, finely chopped
- 4 cups of veggies stock

- 1 cup of half and half
- 1 ounce of dry mushroom
- 2 tablespoons of red wine
- 1 tablespoon of olive oil
- Black pepper
- Salt

Directions:

1. Press the sauté button on the pressure cooker and sauté in it the fresh and dry mushroom for 6 min then add the celery with onion and cook them for 4 min.

2. Stir in the stock with red wine and potato, a pinch of salt and pepper then put on the lid and cook them for 8 min on high pressure.

3. Once the time is up, use the natural method to release the pressure.

4. Stir in the cream and allow the soup to cool down slightly then transfer it to a food processor and blend it smooth.

5. Serve your soup warm and enjoy.

Creamy Sweet Potato Soup

(Prep Time: 15 min | Cooking Time: 8 min | Servings 4)

Ingredients:

- 3 sweet potatoes, peeled and cut into chunks
- 4 cups of veggies stock
- 1 yellow onion, finely chopped
- ½ cup of sour cream
- 1 teaspoon of dry rosemary
- Black pepper

- Salt

Directions:

1. Combine all the ingredients in a pressure cooker then put on the lid and cook it for 8 min on high pressure.

2. Once the time is up, use the natural method to release the pressure.

3. Purée the soup with an immersion blender then serve it warm and enjoy.

Parmesan Risotto

(Prep Time: 15 min | Cooking Time: 30 min | Servings 4)

Ingredients:

- 3 cups of chicken broth
- 1 ½ cup of aborio rice

- 1 cup of white wine
- ½ cup of shallot, finely chopped
- 2 ounces of parmesan cheese, grated
- 2 tablespoons of butter
- 2 cloves of garlic, minced
- Black pepper
- Salt

Directions:

1. Press the sauté button on the pressure cooker and melt the butter in it then sauté the shallot for 5 min.

2. Add the garlic and cook them for another minute then stir in the rice and wine.

3. Sauté the rice until it absorbs the wine for 6 to 10 min then stir in the water with cheese, a pinch of salt and pepper.

4. Put on the lid and bring the pot to pressure then cook it for 8 min on high pressure.

5. Once the time is up, use the natural method to release the pressure.

6. Adjust the seasoning of the risotto then serve it warm and enjoy.

Bell peppers Salad

(Prep Time: 10 min | Cooking Time: 4 min | Servings 2 to 3)

Ingredients:

- 2 yellow bell pepper, seeded and sliced
- 2 red bell peppers, seeded and sliced
- 1 tomato, finely chopped
- 1 tomato, puréed
- 2 cloves of garlic, minced
- Salt

Directions:

1. Stir all the ingredients in a pressure cooker and season them with a pinch of salt.

2. Put on the lid and cook them for 5 min on high pressure.

3. Once the time is up, use the natural method to release the pressure.

4. Serve your salad and enjoy.

Asparagus Risotto

(Prep Time: 15 min | Cooking Time: 20 min | Servings 2 to 3)

Ingredients:

- 1 pound of asparagus, roughly chopped

- 4 cups of water

- 2 cups of aborio rice

- 1 yellow onion, finely chopped

- ¼ cup of dry white wine

- 1 tablespoon of olive oil

- Black pepper

- Salt

Directions:

1. Combine the asparagus with water and a pinch of salt in a pressure cooker then put on the lid and cook it for 12 min on high pressure.

2. Once the time is up, use the natural method to release the pressure.

3. Heat the olive oil in a saucepan and sauté in it the onion for 3 min then add the rice and cook them for 2 min.

4. Add the wine and cook them for 2 min until the rice absorb it then transfer the pressure cooker with the asparagus mix.

5. Season them with a pinch of salt and pepper then put on the lid and cook it for 6 min on high pressure.

6. Once the time is up, use the natural method to release the pressure.

7. Serve your risotto warm and enjoy.

Cheese Burger Pasta

(Prep Time: 15 min | Cooking Time: 5 min | Servings 4)

Ingredients:

- ½ pound of lean beef, minced
- 8 ounces of macaroni
- 1 1/3 cup of beef stock
- 1 cup of cheddar cheese, shredded
- 1 small yellow onion, finely chopped
- ¼ cup of ketchup

- 2 tablespoons of yellow mustard
- Black pepper
- Salt

Directions:

1. Stir the beef with macaroni, stock, onion, ketchup and mustard, a pinch of salt and pepper in a pressure cooker then put on the lid and cook them for 5 min on high pressure.

2. Once the time is up, use the natural method to release the pressure.

3. Serve your macaroni and enjoy.

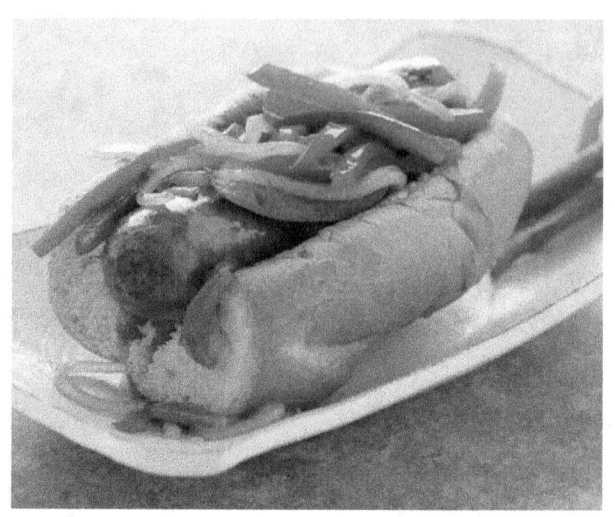

Sausages Sandwiches

(Prep Time: 10 min | Cooking Time: 10 min | Servings 5)

Ingredients:

- 5 sausages

- 15 ounces of canned tomato, diced

- 1 green bell pepper, sliced

- 1 red bell pepper, sliced

- 1 yellow onion, sliced

- 1 teaspoon of Italian herbs

- Black pepper

- Salt

Directions:

1. Place the sausage in the bottom of the pressure cooker then top them with the remaining ingredients.

2. Put on the lid and cook them for 10 min on high pressure.

3. Once the time is up, assemble your sausages and enjoy.

Chicken Spring Rice Casserole

(Prep Time: 12 min | Cooking Time: 6 min | Servings 6)

1Ìngredients:

- 2 chicken breast halves
- 1 can of condensed chicken soup
- 2 cups of frozen mixed veggies
- 1 1/3 cup of water
- ¾ cup of rice
- ½ cup of cheddar cheese, shredded

- ½ teaspoon of onion powder
- Black pepper
- Salt

Directions:

1. Season the chicken with some salt and pepper then stir it with the rice and veggies into the pot.

2. Whisk the soup with water, onion powder, a pinch of salt and pepper then stir them into the pot.

3. Put on the lid and cook them for 18 min on high pressure.

4. Once the time is up, use the natural method to release the pressure.

5. Drain the chicken breasts and set them aside.

6. Transfer the rice and veggies mix to a greased baking dish and place the chicken breasts on top then sprinkle the cheese on them.

7. Grill the chicken rice casserole in the oven for 4 to 6 min or until the cheese melts then serve it and enjoy.

Zuppa Tuscana

(Prep Time: 152 min | Cooking Time: 12 min | Servings 6)

Ingredients:

- 1 pound of hot Italian sausages, casing removed
- 6 cups of chicken broth

- 3 large potatoes, quartered and sliced
- 2 cups of kale
- 1 cup of heavy cream
- ¼ cup of water
- 1 yellow onion, finely chopped
- 1 tablespoon of olive oil
- 3 cloves of garlic, minced
- Black pepper
- Salt

Directions:

1. Press the sauté button on the pressure cooker and heat the oil in it then sauté in it the onion with garlic for 3 min.

2. Add the sausages and sauté them for another 3 min.

3. Stir in the broth with potato, water, a pinch of salt and pepper then put on the lid and cook it for 5 min on high pressure.

4. Once the time is up, use the natural method to release the pressure.

5. Stir in the cream with kale then put on the lid and let the soup set for 5 min then serve it warm and enjoy.

Onion Soup

(Prep Time: 20 min | Cooking Time: 25 min | Servings 6)

Ingredients:

- 1 ½ pound of yellow onion, sliced

- 12 French bread slices

- 6 cups of beef stock

- 1 cup of swiss cheese, grated

- ½ cup of dry white wine

- ¼ cup of butter
- ¼ cup of flour
- 1 tablespoon of vegetable oil
- 1 tablespoon of butter
- Black pepper
- Salt

Directions:

1. Press the sauté button on the pressure cooker and heat the oil and 1 tablespoon of butter in it then sauté in it the onion for 10 min.

2. Stir in the wine and sauté them for 4 min then add the stock with a pinch of salt.

3. Put on the lid and cook the soup for 5 min on high pressure.

4. Once the time is up, use the natural method to release the pressure.

5. In the mea time, melt ¼ cup of butter in a heavy saucepan then add to it the flour gradually while whisking all the time.

6. Add ½ cup of broth from the soup and whisk them until on low heat no lumps are found.

7. Stir the mix back into the soup then press the sauté button and simmer the soup for 6 min.

8. Once the time is up, ladle the soup into heatproof ramekins or bowl and top them with the French bread slices.

9. Sprinkle the cheese on top then grill them in the oven for 2 to 3

min until the cheese melts.

10. Serve your onion soup warm and enjoy.

Black Eyed Sausage Soup

(Prep Time: 1 min | Cooking Time: 20 min | Servings 4 to 6)

Ingredients:

- 28 ounces of canned tomato, diced

- 1 ½ pound of turkey sausages, sliced

- 8 ounces of tomato sauce

- 2 cups of dry black eyed peas

- 2 cups of celery, diced

- 2 cups of carrots, diced
- 3 cups of veggies broth
- 4 collard green leaves, roughly chopped
- ¼ cup of onion, diced
- 1 tablespoon of dry oregano
- 1 tablespoon of olive oil
- 1 tablespoon of chili powder
- 1 teaspoon of cumin
- ½ teaspoon of coriander
- 2 cloves of garlic, minced
- Black pepper
- Salt

Directions:

1. Press the sauté button on the pressure cooker and heat the oil in it then sauté in it the onion with garlic, celery and carrot for 6

min.

2. Stir in the remaining ingredients then season them with some salt and pepper.

3. Put on the lid and cook the soup for 12 min on high pressure.

4. Once the time is up, use the natural method to release the pressure.

5. Serve your soup warm and enjoy.

Garbanzo Macaroni Minestrone

(Prep Time: 15 min | Cooking Time: 20 min | Servings 4)

Ingredients:

- 15 ounces of canned tomato, diced
- 4 cups of water

- 1 carrot, diced
- 1 stalk of celery, diced
- 1 cup of dry chickpeas
- 1 cup of macaroni
- 1 yellow onion, finely chopped
- 1 sprig of fresh sage
- 1 sprig of fresh thyme
- 1 tablespoon of olive oil
- 1 bay leaf
- Black pepper
- Salt

Directions:

1. Press the sauté button on the pressure cooker and heat the oil in it then sauté in it the onion with celery and carrot for 6 min.

2. Stir in the remaining ingredients except for the macaroni then put on the lid and cook them for 14 min on high pressure.

3. Once the time is up, use the natural method to release the pressure.

4. Cook the macaroni according to the directions on the package.

5. Stir the macaroni into the pot then season them with some salt and pepper.

6. Serve your minestrone warm and enjoy.

Tuna Spaghetti

(Prep Time: 15 min | Cooking Time: 5 min | Servings 4)

Ingredients:

- 16 ounces of pasta

- 12 ounces of canned olive oil tuna, drained

- 4 cups of water

- 2 cups of tomato, finely chopped

- 3 anchovies

- 1 tablespoon of olive oil

- 1 clove of garlic, minced

- Water
- Black pepper
- Salt

Directions:

1. Press the sauté button on the pressure cooker and heat the oil in it and sauté in it the anchovies with garlic for 1 min.

2. Stir in the remaining ingredients then put on the lid and cook them for 4 min on low pressure.

3. Once the time is up, use the natural method to release the pressure.

4. Serve your pasta warm and enjoy.

Green Beans Sauté

(Prep Time: 10 min | Cooking Time: 7 min | Servings 4)

Ingredients:

- 1 ½ pounds of green beans, trimmed
- 3 cups of tomato, crushed

- 1 tablespoon of olive oil
- 1 clove of garlic, minced
- Black pepper
- Salt

Directions:

1. Combine all the ingredients in a pressure cooker then season them with some salt and pepper.

2. Put on the lid and cook them for 7 min on high pressure.

3. Once the time is up, use the natural method to release the pressure.

4. Serve your green beans sauté warm and enjoy.

Sesame Chicken Wings

(Prep Time: 15 min | Cooking Time: 16 min | Servings 4)

Ingredients:

- 3 pounds of chicken wings
- 1 cup of teriyaki sauce
- 6 tablespoons of sesame oil
- 2 tablespoons of sugar
- 1 tablespoon of lemon juice
- Black pepper

- Salt

Directions:

1. Toss 4 tablespoons of sesame seeds, chicken wings, lemon juice, sugar, teriyaki sauce, a pinch of salt and pepper in a large zip lock bag then refrigerate them for an overnight.

2. Drain the chicken wings from the marinade.

3. Press the sauté button on the pressure cooker and heat 4

tablespoons of sesame oil in it then brown in it the chicken wings for 6 min.

4. Stir in the remaining marinade then put on the lid and cook it for 10 min on high pressure.

5. Once the time is up, serve your chicken wings warm and enjoy.

Prosciutto Chicken

(Prep Time: 15 min | Cooking Time: 12 min | Servings 6)

Ingredients:

- 6 chicken breasts
- 6 prosciutto slices
- 1 cup of frozen peas
- ¾ cup of chicken stock
- 6 sage leaves
- 1 tablespoon of olive oil

- 1 tablespoon of butter

- Black pepper

- Salt

Directions:

1. Place the chicken breasts between two pieces of parchment paper and pound them until they become flat.

2. Place a prosciutto slice on each chicken breast and roll them then secure them with toothpicks and season them with some salt and pepper.

3. Press the sauté button on the pressure cooker then melt in it the butter with olive oil.

4. Brown in it the chicken rolls for 3 min on each side then stir into them the remaining ingredients.

5. Put on the lid and cook them for 7 min on high pressure.

6. Once the time is up, use the natural method to release the pressure.

7. Serve your chicken rolls warm and enjoy.

Spicy Pressure Bows

(Prep Time: 15 min | Cooking Time: 6 min | Servings 4)

Ingredients:

- 16 ounce of bow-tie pasta
- 15 ounces of canned tomato, diced
- 2 cups of water
- ½ cup of mixed shredded cheese
- 2 tablespoons of olive oil
- ½ teaspoon of dry oregano
- ½ teaspoon of garlic powder
- Black pepper

- Salt

Directions:

1. Press the sauté button on the pressure cooker and heat the oil in it.

2. Stir in the pasta with water, tomato, oregano, garlic powder, a pinch of salt and pepper then put on the lid and cook it for 6 min on low pressure.

3. Once the time is up, use the natural method to release the pressure.

4. Sprinkle the cheese all over the pasta and cover the pot then let it set until the cheese melts.

5. Serve your pasta warm and enjoy.

Chicken Butter

(Prep Time: 15 min | Cooking Time: 21 min | Servings 6)

Ingredients:

- 10 chicken thighs, boneless and skinless, diced

- 28 ounces of canned tomato, diced

- ¾ cup of Greek yogurt

- ¾ cup of heavy cream
- ½ cup of butter
- 2 tablespoons of cold water
- 2 tablespoons of cornstarch
- 2 tablespoons of fresh ginger, minced
- 1 tablespoon of paprika
- 1 teaspoon of cumin
- Black pepper
- Salt

Directions:

1. Press the sauté button on the pressure cooker and melt the butter in it.

2. Brown in it the chicken in batches for 3 min per batch.

3. Stir in the remaining ingredients then season them with some salt and pepper.

4. Put on the lid and cook them for 10 min on high pressure.

5. Once the time is up, use the natural method to release the pressure.

6. Serve your chicken butter warm and enjoy.

Pulled Apple Chicken

(Prep Time: 15 min | Cooking Time: 12 min | Servings 1 to 2)

Ingredients:

- 1 pound of chicken breast
- 2 cups of apple juice
- 1 green apple, quartered
- ½ yellow onion, sliced
- Black pepper
- Salt

Directions:

1. Season the chicken with some salt and pepper then stir it into the pot with the remaining ingredients.

2. Put on the lid and cook it for 12 min on high pressure.

3. Once the time is up, use the natural method to release the pressure.

4. Drain the chicken and shred it.

5. Purée the apple mix in the pot then stir into it the shredded chicken.

6. Serve your apple chicken and enjoy.

Mustard Chicken Curry

(Prep Time: 15 min | Cooking Time: 15 min | Servings 6)

Ingredients:

- 3 pounds of chicken breasts, diced

- 1 pound of golden potatoes, peeled and diced

- ½ cup of water

- ½ cup of heavy cream
- 2 tablespoons of coconut oil
- 1 tablespoon of curry powder
- 1 tablespoon of fresh ginger, peeled and minced
- 1 teaspoon of turmeric
- 1 teaspoon of cumin
- 2 cloves of garlic, minced
- Black pepper
- Salt

Directions:

1. Stir all the ingredients in a pressure cooker then season them with some salt and pepper.

2. Put on the lid and cook them for 15 min on high pressure.

3. Once the time is up, use the natural method to release the pressure.

4. Adjust the seasoning of the curry then serve it warm and enjoy.

Spaghetti Meatballs

(Prep Time: 15 min | Cooking Time: 5 min | Servings 6)

Ingredients:

- 48 ounces of spaghetti sauce

- ½ pound of lean beef, minced

- ½ pound of lean pork, minced

- 8 ounces of noodles

- 1 ½ cup of water

- ½ cup of panko bread crumbs

- ½ cup of mozzarella cheese, shredded

- 1 egg, beaten

- ¼ cup of milk

- 2 tablespoons of dry basil

- 1 tablespoon of Italian herbs

- Black pepper

- Salt

Directions:

1. Mix the milk with pork and beef, bread crumbs, basil and cheese, egg, Italian herbs, a pinch of salt and pepper in a large bowl then shape them into 1 inch meatballs.

2. Pour half of the sauce in the bottom of a pressure cooker then top it with the meatballs and the remaining sauce.

3. Top them with the noodles and pour the water all over them.

4. Put on the lid and cook them for 5 min on high pressure.

5. Once the time is up, use the natural method to release the pressure then serve your spaghetti meatballs warm and enjoy.

Apple Pork Roast

(Prep Time: 15 min | Cooking Time: 15 min | Servings 6)

Ingredients:

- 3 pound pork loin roast

- 1 large apple, cored and sliced

- 1 bunch of fresh sage
- ¾ cup of white wine
- ¼ cup of water
- 1 tablespoons of olive oil
- Black pepper
- Salt

Directions:

1. Season the pork loin with some salt and pepper then make in it several slits and place a slice of apple in each slit.

2. Place the pork loin in a pressure cooker and add to it the remaining ingredients then put on the lid and cook them for 15

min on high pressure.

3. Once the time is up, use the natural method to release the pressure.

4. Serve your pork roast warm and enjoy.

Cottage Pie

(Prep Time: 20 min | Cooking Time: 35 min | Servings 6)

Ingredients:

- 1 ½ pound of potato, sliced
- 1 ½ pounds of lean beef
- 2 large carrots, diced
- 1 yellow onion, finely chopped
- 1 cup of stock

- 1 cup of frozen peas
- ½ cup of milk
- 3 tablespoons of butter
- 1 tablespoon of Worcestershire sauce
- 1 tablespoon of tomato paste
- 1 teaspoon of fresh thyme leaves, finely chopped
- Black pepper
- Salt

Directions:

1. Mix the potato with a pinch of salt.

2. Press the sauté button on the pressure cooker and melt in it 1

tablespoon of butter in it.

3. Add the onion with beef and carrot then sauté them for 6 min.

4. Stir in the stock with Worcestershire sauce, tomato paste, thyme, a pinch of salt and pepper.

5. Lower the steamer basket on top of them then fill it with the potato.

6. Put on the lid and cook them for 12 min on high pressure.

7. Once the time is up, use the natural method to release the pressure.

8. Remove the potato from the steamer basket then mash it with 2

tablespoons of butter and set it aside.

9. Preheat the oven on 400 F.

10. Transfer the cooked beef mix to a greased baking dish then top it with the mashed potato.

11. Bake the cottage pie for uncovered for 20 min then serve it warm and enjoy.

Juicy Chicken Breasts

(Prep Time: 15 min | Cooking Time: 30 min | Servings 6)

Ingredients:

- 6 pound Breasts breast
- 14 ounces of chicken broth

- 1 stalk of celery, diced
- 1 yellow onion, quartered
- 3 tablespoons of cold water
- 3 tablespoons of cornstarch
- Black pepper
- Salt

Directions:

1. Season the Chicken breasts with some salt and **pepper then stir it with the remaining** ingredients into the pot.

2. Put on the lid and cook it for 30 min on high pressure.

3. Once the time is up, use the natural method to release the pressure.

4. Serve your Chicken breasts with some rice and enjoy.

Moroccan Lamb and Prunes Tajine

(Prep Time: 15 min | Cooking Time: 30 min | Servings 6)

Ingredients:

- 3 pounds of lamb shoulder, cut into pieces
- 10 ounces of dry prunes, soaked for 30 min
- 2 yellow onions, sliced
- 1 cup of veggies stock
- 3 tablespoons of vegetable oil
- 3 tablespoons of honey
- 2 cloves of garlic, minced

- 1 teaspoon of ginger
- 1 teaspoon of turmeric
- 1 teaspoon of cinnamon
- 1 teaspoon of cumin
-
- 1 cinnamon stick
- 1 bay leaf
- Black pepper
- Salt

Directions:

1. Stir all the ingredients in a pressure cooker then put on the lid and cook them for 30 min on high pressure.

2. Once the time is up, use the natural method to release the pressure.

3. Discard the bay leaf and cinnamon stick then serve it and enjoy.

Turkey Beans Chili

(Prep Time: 15 min | Cooking Time: 25 min | Servings 4)

Ingredients:

- 2 pounds turkey breast
- 2 cups of dry kidney beans
- 2 cups of bone broth
- 1 cup of tomato, finely chopped

- 1 bell pepper, diced
- 1 yellow onion, finely chopped
- 2 tablespoons of tomato paste
- 2 tablespoons of vegetable oil
- 1 teaspoon of cumin
- ¼ teaspoon of dry thyme
- Black pepper
- Salt

Directions:

1. Press the sauté button on the pot and heat the oil in it then sauté in it the bell pepper with onion for 4 min.

2. Stir in the remaining ingredients then put on the lid and cook them for 25 min on high pressure.

3. Once the time is up, use the natural method to release the pressure.

4. Drain the turkey breast and shred it then stir it back into the pot.

5. Adjust the seasoning of the chili then serve it warm and enjoy

Italian Chicken Marinara

(Prep Time: 15 min | Cooking Time: 20 min | Servings 4)

Ingredients:

- 2 pounds of chicken breasts
- 2 cups of marinara sauce
- ¾ cup of onion, finely chopped
- ½ cup of red bell pepper, finely **chopped**
- 1 tablespoon of olive oil

- black pepper

- Salt

Directions:

1. Press the sauté button on the pressure cooker and heat the oil in it then sauté in it the onion with bell pepper for 4 min.

2. Add the chicken with marinara sauce, a pinch of salt and pepper then put on the lid and cook them for 12 min on high pressure.

3. Once the time is up, use the natural method to release the pressure.

4. Drain the chicken breasts and shred them then stir them back into the pot.

5. Serve your Italian chicken and enjoy.

Honey Chicken

(Prep Time: 15 min | Cooking Time: 12 min | Servings 4)

Ingredients:

- 2 pounds of chicken breasts

- 2/3 cup of teriyaki sauce

- ¼ cup of chicken broth
- 1 tablespoon of honey
- Black pepper
- Salt

Directions:

1. Stir all the ingredients in a pressure cooker then season them with some salt and pepper.

2. Put on the lid and cook them for 12 min on high pressure.

3. Once the time is up, use the natural method to release the pressure.

4. Drain the chicken breasts and shred them then stir them back into the pot.

5. Serve your honey chicken warm and enjoy.

Ranch Chicken

(Prep Time: 15 min | Cooking Time: 12 min | Servings 4)

Ingredients:

- 2 pounds of chicken breasts

- 1 cup of chicken broth

- 4 ounces of cream cheese

- 1 ounces of ranch dressing seasoning
- 1 tablespoon of olive oil
- Black pepper
- Salt

Directions:

1. Combine the chicken with olive oil, broth, ranch dressing, a pinch of salt and pepper then put on the lid and cook them for 12 min on high pressure.

2. Once the time is up, use the natural method to release the pressure then drain the chicken and shred it.

3. Stir the chicken back into the pot with the cream cheese then serve it and enjoy.

Bell Chicken Pasta

(Prep Time: 15 min | Cooking Time: 16 min | Servings 4)

Ingredients:

- 2 pounds of chicken breasts
- 10 ounces of tomato, diced

- 2 red bell peppers, seeded and sliced
- 1 cup of cream cheese
- 2/3 cup of chicken broth
- ½ cup of onion, finely chopped
- 1 tablespoon of olive oil
- 2 teaspoons of garlic powder
- 1 teaspoon of cumin
- Black pepper
- Salt

Directions:

1. Press the sauté button on the pressure cooker and heat the oil in it then sauté in it the bell pepper with onion for 4 min.

2. Stir in the chicken with broth, tomato, cumin, garlic, a pinch of salt and pepper then put on the lid and cook them for 12 min on high pressure.

3. Once the time is up, use the natural method to release the pressure then drain the chicken and shred it.

4. Stir the chicken back into the pot with the cream cheese.

5. Serve your bell chicken with some pasta and enjoy.

Chili Onion Chicken Pasta

(Prep Time: 12 min | Cooking Time: 20 min | Servings 4)

Ingredients:

- 3 pounds of chicken breasts

- 24 ounces of pasta

- 2 small yellow onion, finely chopped

- 1 cup of chicken broth

- 1 cup of canned tomato, crushed
- 1 cup of cream cheese
- ½ tablespoon of garlic, finely chopped
- 1 tablespoon of olive oil
- Black pepper
- Salt

Directions:

1. Press the sauté button on the pressure cooker and heat the oil in it then sauté in it the onion with garlic for 3 min.

2. Stir in the chicken with broth, tomato, a pinch of salt and pepper then put on the lid and cook them for 14 min on high pressure.

3. In the meantime, cook the pasta according to the directions on the package.

4. Once the time is up, use the natural method to release the pressure then drain the chicken and shred it.

5. Stir the chicken back into the pot with the cream cheese and pasta then serve it warm and enjoy.

Corny Chicken Pasta

(Prep Time: 15 min | Cooking Time: 8 min | Servings 4)

Ingredients:

- 14.5 ounces of canned tomato, roasted

- 1 ½ cup of macaroni

- 1 ½ cup of veggies broth

- ½ cup of corn kernels

- ½ cup of water

- 1 small yellow onion, diced

- ¼ cup of nutritional yeast

- ¼ cup of mozzarella cheese, crumbled

- 1 teaspoon of canola oil
- 1 teaspoon of garlic, minced
- Black pepper
- Salt

Directions:

1. Press the sauté button on the pressure cooker and heat the oil in it then sauté in it the onion with garlic for 2 min.

2. Stir in the remaining ingredients except for the cheese then put on the lid and cook them for 5 min on low pressure.

3. Once the time is up, use the natural method to release the pressure.

4. Stir in the mozzarella cheese then serve your macaroni stew and enjoy.

Loaded Chicken Soup

(Prep Time: 15 min | Cooking Time: 20 min | Servings 6)

Ingredients:

- 1 pound of chicken breasts, diced
- 6 carrots, sliced
- 1 pound of celery, diced
- 1 pound of potato, diced

- 6 cups of chicken broth

- 1 yellow onion, finely chopped

- 3 tablespoons of olive oil

- Black pepper

- Salt

Directions:

1. Press the sauté button on the pressure cooker and heat the oil in it then sauté in it the onion for 4 min.

2. Stir in the remaining ingredients then put on the lid and cook them for 15 min on high pressure.

3. Once the time is up, adjust the seasoning of the soup then serve it warm and enjoy.

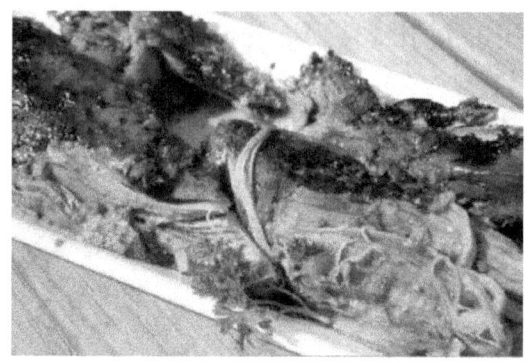

Chipotle Brisket

(Prep Time: 15 min | Cooking Time: 55 min | Servings 6)

Ingredients:

- 4 pounds brisket

- 24 ounces of barbecue sauce

- ½ cup of water

- 3 tablespoons of chipotle sauce

- 2 tablespoons of olive oil

- 2 teaspoons of paprika

- 2 cloves of garlic, minced

- Black pepper

- Salt

Directions:

1. Season the brisket with some salt and pepper.

2. Press the sauté button on the pressure cooker and heat the oil in it then brown in it the brisket for 4 min on each side.

3. Whisk the water with barbecue sauce, paprika, garlic and chipotle sauce in a large bowl then pour it all over the brisket.

4. Put on the lid and cook the brisket for 45 min on high pressure.

5. Once the time is up, use the natural method to release the pressure.

6. Serve your brisket warm and enjoy.

Shredded Beef Burgers

(Prep Time: 20 min | Cooking Time: 40 min | Servings 6)

Ingredients:

- 3 pounds of pork butt
- 2 cups of apple cider
- 2 tablespoons of apple cider vinegar
- Black pepper

- Salt

Directions:

1. Season the pork butt with some salt and pepper then stir it into a pressure cooker with the remaining ingredients.

2. Put on the lid and cook it for 40 min on high pressure.

3. Once the time is up, drain the pork butt and shred it then serve it some barbecue sauce and enjoy.

Greek Style Stew

(Prep Time: 15 min | Cooking Time: 30 min | Servings 4)

Ingredients:

- 2 pounds of beef meat
- 28 ounces of canned tomato, diced
- 2 carrots, diced
- 1 pound of baby potatoes, peeled
- 1 yellow onion, finely chopped

- ½ cup of beef broth
- ½ cup of water
- ¼ cup of red wine
- 1 tablespoon of olive oil
- 1 ½ teaspoon of brown sugar
- 1 teaspoon of cumin
- ½ teaspoon of dry rosemary
- 1/8 teaspoon of cinnamon
- Black pepper
- Salt

Directions:

1. Heat the oil in a pressure cooker and press the sauté button then sauté in it the onion for 4 min.

2. Stir in the carrot with rosemary and red wine then sauté them for another 4 min.

3. Stir in the remaining ingredients then season them with some salt and pepper.

4. Put on the lid and bring the pot to pressure then cook it for 16

min on high pressure.

5. Once the time is up, use the natural method to release the pressure.

6. Drain the beef and shred it then stir it back into the pot.

7. Adjust the seasoning of the stew then serve it warm and enjoy.

Brisket Pot

(Prep Time: 15 min | Cooking Time: 45 min | Servings 6)

Ingredients:

- 3 pounds brisket

- 1 cup of beef stock
- ¾ cup of red wine
- ½ cup o f barbecue sauce
- 1 packet of onion soup mix
- 2 tablespoons of brown sugar
- 1 tablespoon of vegetable oil
- 2 teaspoons of Worcestershire sauce
- 1 teaspoon of dry thyme
- ¼ teaspoon of onion powder
- ¼ teaspoon of garlic powder
- Black pepper
- Salt

Directions:

1. Season the brisket with some salt and pepper.

2. Combine all the ingredients in a pressure cooker and whisk them until they become smooth then add the brisket and put on the lid.

3. Bring the pot to pressure and cook them for 45 min on high pressure.

4. Once the time is up, use the natural method to release the pressure.

5. Drain the brisket and shred it then stir it back into the pot.

6. Serve your shredded brisket warm and enjoy.

Flat Brisket with Gravy

(Prep Time: 12 min | Cooking Time: 35 min | Servings 4)

Ingredients:

- 3 pounds flat brisket

- 2 cups of red wine
- 2 cups of stock
- 1 cup of gravy
- 4 tablespoons of vegetable oil
- 1 tablespoon of tomato purée
- 2 thyme sprigs
- Black pepper
- Salt

Directions:

1. Season the brisket with some salt and pepper then place it in a pressure cooker with the red wine, stock, oil, tomato purée and thyme sprigs.

2. Put on the lid and cook it for 35 min on high pressure.

3. Once the time is up, use the natural method to release the pressure.

4. Serve your flat brisket with the gravy and enjoy.

Wine Pears

(Prep Time: 15 min | Cooking Time: 12 min | Servings 6)

Ingredients:

- 6 fresh pears, peeled
- 1 bottle of red wine
- 2 cups of sugar
- 1 stick of cinnamon
- 4 cloves
- 1 teaspoon of fresh ginger, finely chopped

Directions:

1. Whisk the wine with sugar, cloves, cinnamon stick and ginger in a pressure cooker then lower in it the pears.

2. Put on the lid and cook the pears for 7 min on high pressure.

3. Once the time is up, use the natural method to release the pressure.

4. Drain the pears and set them aside.

5. Press the sauté button and cook the liquid in the pot until it reduces slightly then serve it with the pears and enjoy.

Chocolate Cake

(Prep Time: 15 min | Cooking Time: 35 min | Servings 6)

Ingredients:

- 1 cup of purpose flour
- ½ cup of sugar
- ½ and ¼ cup of water
- ¼ cup of butter
- ¼ cup of vegetable oil
- ¼ cup of cocoa powder
- ¼ cup of yogurt
- 1 teaspoon of vanilla extract
- 1 teaspoon of vinegar
- ½ teaspoon of baking soda
- ¼ teaspoon of Salt

Directions:

1. Mix the sugar with salt and flour in a mixing bowl and set it aside.

2. Combine the oil with butter, ½ cup of water and cocoa powder in a heavy saucepan and stir them on low heat until no lumps are found.

3. Transfer the mix to the flour mix bowl and whisk them until they become smooth.

4. Whisk the yogurt with ¼ cup of water, baking soda, vinegar and vanilla then add them to the flour mix and whisk them until no lumps are found.

5. Pour 1 cup of salt in the bottom of a pressure cooker and lower a steaming rack in it.

6. Pour the batter into a greased and lined up baking pan and place it on the rack.

7. Put on the lid and cook the cake for 35 min on high pressure.

8. Once the time is up, use the natural method to release the pressure then set the cake aside to cool down completely.

9. Serve your cake and enjoy.

Apple Cake

(Prep Time: 15 min | Cooking Time: 15 min | Servings 6)

Ingredients:

- 2 cups of water
- 1 cup of purpose flour
- 1 cup of ricotta cheese
- 1/3 cup of sugar
- ¼ cup of raw sugar
- 1 apple, peeled and sliced
- 1 apple, peeled and diced
- 1 egg
- 3 tablespoons of olive oil
- 1 tablespoon of fresh lemon juice
- 2 teaspoons of baking powder
- 1 teaspoon of baking soda
- 1/8 teaspoon of cinnamon powder

- Salt

Directions:

1. Toss the sliced and diced apples with lemon juice in a mixing bowl.

2. Sprinkle the raw sugar in the bottom of a greased and lined up baking pan then lay the apple slices on it.

3. Mix the sugar with ricotta cheese, baking soda, baking powder and olive oil, egg, cinnamon, flour and a pinch of salt in a large mixing bowl until they become smooth.

4. Stir in the diced apple then pour the batter all over the apple slices.

5. Pour 2 cups of water in the bottom of a pressure cooker and lower in it a steamer rack then place the cake pan on it.

6. Put on the lid and cook the cake for 15 min on high pressure.

7. Once the time is up, use the natural method to release the pressure.

8. Serve your cake and enjoy.

Christmas Pudding

(Prep Time: 15 min | Cooking Time: 35 min | Servings 8)

Ingredients:

- 1 cup of raw sugar

- 1 cup of purpose flour

- 2/3 cup of dry apricots, finely chopped

- 2/3 cup of dry cranberries

- 4 eggs

- 15 tablespoons of butter, unsalted

- 1 carrot, grated

- 3 tablespoons of maple syrup
- 1 teaspoon of baking powder
- 1 teaspoon of ginger powder
- Salt

Directions:

1. Combine the apricots with cranberries in a bowl and cover them with some boiling water then let them set for 30 min then drain them.

2. Combine the butter with purpose flour, ginger, baking powder and a pinch of salt in a food processor and pulse them few times.

3. Add the maple syrup with eggs and blend them smooth again.

4. Pour the batter into a large mixing bowl and fold into it then dry fruits with the carrot.

5. Pour 2 cups of water in a pressure cooker and lower in it a steamer basket.

6. Pour the batter into a greased pudding pan then place it on the rack.

7. Put on the lid and cook the pudding for 35 min on high pressure.

8. Once the time is up, use the natural method to release the pressure and let the pudding cool down in the pot for 20 min.

9. Serve your pudding and enjoy.

Part 2

Introduction

This book has 50 simple and healthy pressure cooker recipes for you to try.

Although many of us love good food, what's unfortunate is that most people shy from cooking because of the time one has to put into preparing a great meal. However, this does not always have to be the case. If you have heard about a pressure cooker, you know what I am talking about.

While most people know about pressure cookers, interestingly, most don't know much about this all-important appliance. To help you understand how good pressure cookers are, just think for a second; cutting down your cooking time from 2 hours to 30 minutes, isn't that amazing?

This is what pressure cookers do. They cut cooking time to almost half and you not only save energy in the process but also time. While you may know how good pressure cookers are, most people just assume they are good for cooking legumes, grains and meat. However, there is much more that you can do with a pressure cooker. This book has 50 recipes that you can try to unleash the power of a pressure cooker.

Thanks again for downloading this book, I hope you enjoy it!

Breakfast Recipes

1. Pressure Cooker Quinoa

Servings: 6

Ingredients

2 ¼ cups of water

½ teaspoon of vanilla

Pinch of salt

1 ½ cups of uncooked quinoa, well rinsed

2 tablespoons of maple syrup

¼ teaspoon of ground cinnamon

Optional Toppings: fresh berries, milk, sliced almonds

Directions

Add vanilla, maple syrup, water, quinoa, salt, and cinnamon to the pressure cooking pot.

Set the pressure to high, and select one minute cooking time.

Once the beep sounds, turn off the pressure cooker, and then wait for ten minutes before using a Quick Pressure Release to get rid of the remaining pressure.

Remove the lid once the valve drops gently, and tilt it away from you to allow the steam to escape.

Fluff quinoa, and serve immediately with sliced almonds, berries, and milk.

2. Apple Cinnamon Steel Cut Oats

Servings: 3

Ingredients

1 cup of steel cut oats

1 large apple, peeled, cored and diced

1 ½ teaspoons of ground cinnamon

1 tablespoon of butter

3 ½ cups of water

2 tablespoons of light brown sugar

¼ teaspoon of salt

Directions

Place butter into your pressure cooking pot, and select sauté. Wait for the butter to melt before adding the toast and oats, stirring constantly until the mixture darkens and starts to smell nutty, approximately three minutes.

Add brown sugar, apples, water, salt and cinnamon. Set the pressure to high, and select ten minutes cooking time.

Wait for the beep to sound, turn the pressure cooker off, and then apply a natural pressure release for ten minutes. Release the remaining pressure using a quick pressure release.

Remove the lid when the valve drops carefully, stir the oats, then cover and set aside for five to ten minutes or until the oats achieve the desired thickness.

Top with additional brown sugar, nuts, and milk, if so desired.

3. Carrot Cake Oatmeal

Servings: 6

Ingredients

1 cup of steel cut oats

1 cup of grated carrots

2 teaspoons of cinnamon

1 tablespoon of butter

¼ teaspoon of salt

¼ cup of chia seeds

4 cups of water

3 tablespoons of maple syrup

1 teaspoon of pumpkin pie spice

¾ cup of raisins

Directions

Add butter into the pressure cooking pot, and select sauté. Wait for the butter to melt, and then mix in the toast and oats, stirring constantly until the mixture smells nutty, approximately three minutes.

Add pumpkin pie spice, cinnamon, maple syrup, carrots, water, and salt. Set the pressure to high, and select ten minutes cooking time.

When the beep sounds, turn the pressure cooker off. Apply a natural pressure release for ten minutes, followed by a quick pressure release to get rid of the remaining pressure. Remove the lid once the valve drops carefully.

Stir the oats, and then mix in the chia seeds and raisins. Cover and leave the mixture to sit for five to ten minutes or until the oats achieved the desired thickness.

Top with milk, chopped nuts, maple syrup, and additional raisins.

4. Pumpkin Oats With Pecan Pie Granola

Servings: 6

Ingredients

1 cup of steel cut oats

1 cup of pumpkin puree

2 teaspoons of cinnamon

¼ teaspoon of salt

1 tablespoon of butter

3 cups of water

¼ cup of maple syrup

1 teaspoon of pumpkin pie spice

Directions

Add butter into the pressure cooking pot, and select sauté. Wait until the butter has melted before adding the toast and oats, stirring constantly until the mixture smells nutty, approximately three minutes.

Add pumpkin pie spice, cinnamon, maple syrup, pumpkin puree, water, and salt. Set the pressure to high, and select ten minutes cooking time.

Once you hear the beep, turn the pressure cooker off, and apply a natural pressure release for ten minutes, followed by a quick pressure release to get rid of the remaining pressure. Remove the lid once the valve drops.

Stir the oats, and set the cooking pot aside, uncovered, for five to ten minutes, or until it reaches desired consistency.

Serve with maple syrup, milk, and pecan pie granola, if desired.

5. Pressure Cooker Cinnamon Bread Pudding With Caramel Pecan Sauce

Servings: 6

Ingredients

½ cup of packed brown sugar

3 eggs, beaten

½ teaspoon of ground cinnamon

7 (¾ inch) thick slices of cinnamon bread, cubed and toasted

4 tablespoons butter, melted

3 cups whole milk

1 teaspoon vanilla extract

¼ teaspoon salt

½ cup raisins

Caramel Pecan Sauce

¼ cup of corn syrup

2 tablespoons of butter

1 teaspoon of vanilla extract

¾ cup of brown sugar

2 tablespoons of heavy cream

½ teaspoon of salt

½ cup pecans, toasted & coarsely chopped

Directions

Whisk together the cinnamon, vanilla, beaten eggs, milk, brown sugar, melted butter, and salt in a large bowl. Stir in the raisins and cubed bread. Set the mixture aside for twenty minutes, or until all the milk has been absorbed, making sure that you stir occasionally.

Transfer the bread pudding into a buttered metal baking dish or 1 ½ quart glass. Cover the dish with an aluminum foil, and prepare a sling to remove the dish from the pressure cooking pot by folding an eighteen-inch strip of foil lengthwise twice.

Add one and a half cups of water into the cooking pot, and place it at the bottom. Place the dish at the center of the foil strip before lowering it into the pressure cooker.

Seal properly with the lid, set the pressure to high, and select twenty minutes on the timer. Turn the pressure cooker off when the beep sounds, and apply a quick pressure release to get rid of the remaining pressure. Remove the lid when the valve drops carefully.

Remove the dish, and slide it into a preheated 350 degree F oven for five to ten minutes, or until the top is crispy (optional).

Preparing the caramel pecan sauce

Combine the butter, heavy cream, corn syrup, brown sugar, and salt in a small saucepan. Bring the mixture to a boil over medium high heat, while stirring constantly. Lower the heat, and continue simmering until the sauce is smooth and all the sugar has been absorbed. Stir in the chopped pecans and vanilla.

6. Blueberry Lemon Oats

Servings: 6

Ingredients

1 cup of steel cut oats

½ cup of half and half

1 tablespoon of lemon zest

1 cup of fresh or frozen blueberries

1 tablespoon of butter

3 cups of water

2 tablespoons of sugar

¼ teaspoon of salt

¼ cup of chia seeds

Directions

Add butter into the pressure cooking pot, and select sauté. Wait for the butter to melt before adding the toast and oats, stirring constantly, approximately three minutes.

Add zest, sugar, half and half, water, and salt. Set the pressure to high, and select ten minutes cooking time.

Wait for the beep to sound, and then turn the pressure cooker off. Apply a natural pressure release for ten minutes, followed by a quick pressure release to get rid of the remaining pressure. Remove the lid carefully once the valve drops.

Stir the oats, and then mix in the chia seeds and blueberries. Cover and set aside for five minutes, or until the oats reach desired thickness.

Top with a splash of milk, sliced almonds, agave or honey, and additional blueberries.

7. Tapioca Pudding

Servings: 4

Ingredients

1 ½ cups of water

½ cup of sugar

2 egg yolks

½ cup of small-pearl tapioca

½ cup of whole milk

¼ teaspoon of salt

½ teaspoon of vanilla extract

Directions

Mix together water and the tapioca in a pressure cooking pot. Secure the lid, set the pressure to high and select six minutes in the timer. Wait for ten minutes before applying a quick pressure release to get rid of the remaining pressure.

Whisk together the salt and sugar into the tapioca.

Mix together the milk and egg yolks in a small mixing bowl, and pass through a fine mesh strainer into the pressure cooking pot. Set sauté and cook while stirring constantly until the mixture starts to boil. Turn the pressure cooker off and mix in the vanilla.

Cool the mixture to room temperature while stirring occasionally. Transfer into serving dishes and place in the refrigerator to chill.

8. Breakfast Rice pudding

Servings: 4
Ingredients

1 ½ cups of water

2 cups of whole milk, divided

2 eggs

¾ cup of raisins

1 cup of Arborio rice

¼ teaspoon of salt

½ cup of sugar

½ teaspoon of vanilla extract

Directions

Combine the water, rice, and salt in a pressure cooking pot. Secure the lid, set the pressure to high, and select three minutes cooking time. Wait for the beep to sound, and then turn the pressure cooker off. Apply a natural pressure release for ten minutes, and then a quick pressure release to get rid of the remaining pressure.

Whisk together the vanilla, remaining half cup of milk, and eggs in a small mixing bowl. Sieve through a fine mess strainer into the cooking pot. Set sauté and cook while stirring constantly until the mixture starts boiling. Turn the pressure cooker off, and take out the cooking pot. Stir in the raisins.

Serve warm or chill until ready to serve. Top with whipped cream and sprinkle with nutmeg or cinnamon, if desired.

9. Peaches And Creamy Oats

Servings: 4

Ingredients

1 cups of steel cut oats

2 cups of water

2 diced peaches

1 cup full of fat coconut milk

½ vanilla bean scraped – seeds and pod added to pressure cooker.

Directions

Add all the ingredients to the cooking pot of your pressure cooker. Select high pressure and three minutes cooking time. Allow ten minutes for natural pressure release, and sweeten as needed.

Soup Recipes

10. Sweet Potato Cheese soup

Servings: 6 – 8

Ingredients

½ cup of chopped onion

1 teaspoon of salt

1/8 teaspoon of red pepper flakes

3 cups of peeled and cubed sweet potatoes

2 tablespoons of cornstarch

3 oz. of cream cheese, cubed

2 cups of half and half

6 slices of crumbled crisp-cooked bacon

2 tablespoons of butter

2 (14 ounce) cans of chicken broth

½ teaspoon of black pepper

2 tablespoons of dried parsley

3 cups of peeled & cubed russet potatoes

2 tablespoons of water

1 cup of shredded cheddar cheese

1 cup of frozen corn

Directions

Choose sauté on the pressure cooker and add butter into the cooker pot. Once the butter has melted, mix in the onion and cook while stirring constantly for five minutes, or until the onion is tender. Stir in the parsley, red pepper flakes, pepper, salt, and chicken broth.

Place the steamer basket into the pressure cooker pot, and add the sweet potatoes. Secure the lid, set the pressure to high, and select two minutes cooking time. Once the beep sounds, turn the pressure off and apply a quick pressure release. Remove the sweet potatoes carefully and set aside.

Add russet potatoes into the steamer basket. Secure the lid, set the pressure to high, and select four minutes cooking time. Wait for the beeper to sound, turn the pressure off, and apply a quick pressure release. Remove the steamer basket and potatoes carefully out of the cooking pot.

Dissolve cornstarch in two tablespoons of water in a small bowl. Choose simmer, add cornstarch mixture, and cook while stirring constantly. Add the shredded cheese and cubed cream cheese. Stir until the mixture has melted, and then add the corn, half-and-half, and the remaining chicken broth. Heat these but not to a boil, and then add the potatoes and crumbled bacon.

11. Butternut Squash Soup With Chicken

Yields: 2 ½ quarts

Ingredients

3 tablespoons of butter

½ cup of celery, diced

1 garlic clove, minced

1 14.5 oz. can of diced tomatoes with juice

1/8 teaspoon of dried red pepper flakes

1/8 teaspoon of freshly grated nutmeg

1 cup of chicken, cooked and diced

Green onion tops, thinly sliced

1 ½ lbs. of fresh baked butternut squash

½ cup of green onions, diced

½ cup of carrots, diced

2 14.5 oz. cans of chicken broth

½ teaspoon of Italian seasoning

¼ teaspoon of freshly ground black pepper

1 cup of orzo, cooked

1 ½ cup of half and half

Directions

Melt butter in the pressure cooker pot. Sauté the carrots, celery, and onions. Stir in garlic, and add the squash, tomatoes, and chicken stock. Mix in the nutmeg, pepper, red pepper flakes, and Italian seasoning.

Set the pressure to high, and select ten minutes on the timer. Wait for the beep to sound before turning the pressure cooker off. Leave it for ten minutes and then apply a quick pressure release to get rid of the remaining pressure.

Remove the lid when the valve drops, tilting it away from your side to allow the steam to diffuse.

Puree using an immersion blender until smooth.

Choose simmer, add the half & half, orzo, and chicken, and heat until the chicken is heated through

Garnish with a swirl of half & half, and thin slices of green onions.

12. Pressure Cooker Mushroom Stock

Yields: 3 cups

Ingredients

2 carrots, peeled, trimmed and roughly chopped

2 sprigs fresh thyme

4 cups of water

2 ounces of dried Shiitake mushrooms

2 celery stalks, roughly chopped

2 bay leaves

Directions

Pass the mushrooms under cool running water to eliminate sand or grit. Put all the ingredients in the pressure cooking pot then seal and secure the lid. Set the pressure to high, and select twenty minutes cooking time.

Wait for the beep, then turn off the pressure cooker and apply a natural pressure release.

Pass the stock over a fine mesh strainer and get rid of the solids. Serve immediately, freeze for up to three months, or store in the fridge for two to three days.

13. Pressure Cooker Chicken, And Chorizo Soup

Servings: 6

Ingredients

9 ounces of pork chorizo, casing removed

2 medium onions, chopped

4 cups of chicken broth

2 bay leaves

5 ounces of baby kale

Coarse salt and pepper

2 tablespoons of olive oil, divided

4 boneless skinless chicken thighs, diced

4 garlic chopped or pressed cloves

1 (15-ounce) can of diced tomatoes

3 medium peeled and diced Yukon gold potatoes

1 (15-ounce) can of drained & rinsed garbanzos (chick peas)

Directions

Select the browning setting and preheat the pressure cooker pot. Add one tablespoon of oil, and then mix in the onion, chicken, and chorizo. Cook while stirring occasionally for five minutes, or until the onion is tender. Stir in garlic and cook for one more minute.

Add bay leaves, tomatoes, and chicken broth into the pressure cooker pot, and stir to mix. Add the browned chicken, chorizo, kale, and potatoes.

Secure the lid, set the pressure to high, and select four minutes cooking time. Wait for the beep, turn the pressure cooker off, and then apply a quick pressure release. Remove the lid carefully and remove the bay leaves. Mix in the garbanzo beans, and season with salt and pepper.

14. Creamy Wild Rice And Chicken Soup

Servings: 6-8

Ingredients

1 cup of chopped onion

1 cup of diced celery

2 large uncooked & diced boneless skinless chicken breasts

1 teaspoon of salt

Dash red pepper flakes

2 tablespoons of cornstarch

4 oz. of cream cheese, cut into cubes

1 cup of half and half

2 tablespoons of butter

1 cup of diced carrots

2 14 oz. cans of chicken broth

6 oz. package long grain & wild rice

½ teaspoon of black pepper

1 tablespoon of dried parsley

2 tablespoons of water

1 cup of milk

Directions

Sauté butter in the pressure cooker pot, and then add celery, carrot, and onion. Cook while stirring occasionally until tender, approximately five minutes.

Add parsley, pepper, salt, wild rice, chicken, and chicken broth into the pot

Secure the lid, set the pressure to high, and select five minutes cooking time. Wait for the beep, and then turn the pressure cooker off. Wait five minutes before applying a quick pressure release.

Dissolve cornstarch in two tablespoons of water in a small bowl. Simmer the mixture in the pressure cooker pot while stirring constantly. Stir in cubed cream cheese until it melts completely. Add half & half and milk, and heat the mixture, but not to a boil.

15. Tomato Parmesan soup

Servings: 8

Ingredients

1 large onion, diced

1 large carrot, diced

2 14.5 oz. cans of chicken broth

¼ cup of fresh basil

½ teaspoon of salt

½ cup of shredded Parmesan cheese

3 tablespoons of butter

2 stalks celery, diced

2 garlic cloves, minced or pressed

3 pounds of tomatoes - cored, peeled, & quartered

1 tablespoon of tomato paste

½ teaspoon of freshly ground black pepper

1 cup of half and half

Directions

Melt butter in the pressure cooker pot, and then sauté the carrots, celery, and onions until tender. Mix in the garlic and cook while stirring often for one minute. Add tomato paste, basil, tomatoes, chicken stock, salt and pepper.

Set the pressure to high, and select five minutes cooking time. Wait for the beep and then turn off the pressure cooker. Wait five minutes and then apply a Quick pressure release to get rid of the remaining pressure.

Remove the lid when the valve drops, and puree the mixture until smooth.

Set to Simmer, and mix in the half & half and Parmesan.

16. Pressure Cooker Garden minestrone soup

Servings: 8

Ingredients

1 large onion finely chopped

1 stalk celery, diced

1 small zucchini, chopped

3 lbs. of tomatoes, peeled, seeded & chopped

1 cup of uncooked ditalini pasta

1 teaspoon of salt

1 14.5 oz. can of kidney beans

½ teaspoon of freshly ground black pepper

1 tablespoon of olive oil

2 large carrots, diced

1 cup of fresh corn kernels (about 2 ears)

4 cloves garlic minced

2 (14.5 oz) cans of chicken broth

1 teaspoon of Italian seasoning

2 cups of baby spinach

2 tablespoons of fresh basil, chopped

1 cup (4 ounces) of grated Asiago cheese

Directions

Sauté the oil in the pressure cooker pot, and then cook the onion while stirring occasionally until tender, approximately five minutes. Mix in the garlic, zucchini, corn, celery, carrots, and garlic. Continue cooking while stirring for about five more minutes.

Add the Italian seasoning, pasta, chicken broth, tomatoes, and salt, and secure the lid. Set the pressure to high and select four minutes cooking time. Wait for the beep, and then turn off the pressure cooker. Wait five minutes and then apply a quick pressure release.

Add the basil, beans, and spinach, and season with pepper. Serve topped with cheese.

17. Chicken Noodle Soup

Servings: 6

Ingredients

1 large onion, diced

1 celery rib, diced

2 cups of diced chicken

Freshly ground pepper

1 tablespoon of butter

4 carrots, peeled and cut into ¼-inch-thick rounds

6 cups of chicken stock

1 teaspoon of salt

Egg noodles, cooked

Directions

Sauté butter in the pressure cooker pot, and then cook the onion while stirring occasionally until soft, about one to two minutes. Stir in the celery and carrots and sauté for five minutes while stirring occasionally.

Add the chicken and chicken stock, and secure with the lid. Set the pressure to high, and select five minutes. Wait for the beeper, let it sit for five minutes, and then apply a quick pressure release. Remove the lid carefully when the valve drops. Season with salt and pepper.

Serve with the prepared noodles.

18. Chicken Stock

Servings: 8 cups

Ingredients

1 large onion, coarsely chopped

2 celery stalks, roughly chopped

1 bay leaf

3 sprigs fresh thyme

8 cups of water

4 lb whole chicken

2 large carrots, roughly chopped

3 garlic cloves, smashed

5 sprigs fresh parsley

½ teaspoon of whole peppercorns

Directions

Add all the ingredients into the pressure cooker pot, set the pressure to high and select twenty minutes on the timer. Once the beeper sounds, turn off the pressure cooker and apply a natural pressure release. Remove the lid carefully when the valve drops.

Set the stock aside to cool slightly, and then pass it through a fine mesh strainer into a pot or large bowl. Discard the herbs, vegetables, skin, meat, and bones. Cover and slide into the refrigerator. Once chilled, remove the fat from surface.

19. Pressure Cooker Portobello Mushroom And Barley Soup

Servings: 6-8

Ingredients

½ yellow onion, diced

2 carrots, diced

2 large portobello mushrooms, sliced

¾ cup of pearled barley (dry), rinsed and drained

4 cups of water

Salt & pepper to taste

Avocado oil (or your preferred vegetable oil, optional)

2 cloves garlic, minced

3 celery stalks, diced

1 tomato, diced

3 cups of vegetable stock

2 thyme sprigs

Directions

Heat oil in a pressure cooker pot (uncovered), and sauté onion and garlic for a few minutes.

Stir in carrot and celery and sauté for three to five minutes.

Mix in the stock, barley, tomato, mushrooms, water & thyme

Cover and set the pressure to high. Cook for twenty minutes, and then remove from heat. Release the pressure through a natural pressure release. Add salt and pepper to taste.

Main Dishes

20. Spinach And Whole-Wheat Fusilli

Servings: 8

Ingredients

4 cups of frozen chopped spinach (unthawed)

4 minced cloves garlic, to taste

4 tablespoons of butter, cut into cubes

1 pound of whole-wheat fusilli pasta

5 cups of water

Salt, pepper to taste

½ cup of Parmesan cheese, grated, additional for serving

Directions

Transfer pasta into an instant pressure cooker bowl, and fill it with water, approximately five cups. Top with frozen spinach and garlic.

Cook under high pressure for six minutes.

Apply quick pressure release, then open the lid and stir in Parmesan cheese, butter, salt, and pepper.

Cover again and let it sit for five minutes. Add more parmesan cheese at the top and serve.

21. Pressure Cooker Rice And Lentil Pilaf

Servings: 4-6

Ingredients

Rice & lentils: soak these for thirty minutes before cooking

¼ cup brown rice

½ cup black or green lentils

¼ cup black/wild rice

Vegetables:

½ medium onion, finely chopped

3 cloves garlic, pressed/minced

1 cup sliced mushrooms

1 stalk celery, finely chopped

1 teaspoon of fennel seeds

1 bay leaf

¼ teaspoon of red pepper flakes

1 tablespoon of Italian seasoning blend (unsalted)

1 teaspoon of dried coriander

½ teaspoon of ground black pepper

2 cups of vegetable broth

Directions

Mix the rice and lentils in a medium size bowl and fill with water. Let it soak for thirty minutes, and then drain and rinse thoroughly.

Sauté the vegetables in the pressure cooker over high heat for three to five minutes.

Drain the rice and lentils, and add them to the pressure cooker, along with the vegetable broth and spices.

Secure the lid, set the pressure to high, and select nine minutes cooking time. Wait for the beeper and then allow the pressure to drop naturally.

Stir pilaf once the pressure has been released. If there is some liquid, let the pilaf sit for five minutes while uncovered before you serve so that it can absorb the liquid. Serve with steamed or fresh vegetables.

22. Pressure Cooker Pulled BBQ Beef Sandwiches

Servings: 4 to 6

Ingredients

2 cups of water

½ cup of your favorite BBQ Sauce

1/3 cup of Worcestershire Sauce

1 tablespoon of mustard

2 pounds of beef

4 cups of finely shredded cabbage

1 cup of ketchup

1 tablespoon of horseradish

Directions

Add all the ingredients into your instant pot and stir well. Adjust the setting to "meat" (thirty-five minutes). When done, set aside until the steam subsides. Remove the lid, take the beef out, and shred it. Take it back into the sauce, then simmer until set using the "Sauté" setting.

23. Chicken Pumpkin Corn Chowder

Servings: 4-6

Ingredients

1 cup of diced onion

2 14.5 oz. cans of chicken broth

½ teaspoon of Italian seasoning

1/8 teaspoon of dried red pepper flakes

2 large russet potatoes, cubed

2 cups of frozen corn

2 tablespoons of butter

1 garlic clove, minced

1 15-ounce can of Pumpkin Puree

¼ teaspoon of freshly ground black pepper

1/8 teaspoon of freshly grated nutmeg

2 large skinless boneless chicken breasts, uncooked & diced

½ cup of half and half

Directions

Melt butter in the pressure cooker pot, and then cook the onion while stirring occasionally until tender, around five minutes. Stir in garlic and cook for one more minute.

Add nutmeg, red pepper flakes, pepper, Italian seasoning, pumpkin puree, and chicken broth into the pressure cooker pot.

Stir in the diced chicken and diced potatoes, secure the lid, set the pressure to high, and select four minutes cooking time. Wait for the beep, turn the pressure cooker off, and then apply a quick pressure release.

Mix in the half & half, and corn, and season with salt and pepper.

Top with chopped parsley and crumbled bacon (optional), and serve.

24. Pressure Cooker Spicy Honey Chicken

Servings: 4 to 6

Ingredients

½ teaspoon of dried minced garlic

¾ cup of soy sauce

¾ cup of honey

2 tablespoons of water

3 pounds of boneless, skinless chicken thighs

1 teaspoons of chili garlic sauce

¾ cup of ketchup

2 tablespoons of cornstarch

1 tablespoon of chopped fresh basil

Directions

Add honey, ketchup, soy sauce, chili sauce, and garlic into the pressure cooker pot. Stir in the chicken and cover the pot.

Set the pressure to high, and select nine minutes cooking time.

When the time's up, turn the pressure cooker off and apply a quick pressure release

Dissolve cornstarch in two tablespoons of water in a small bowl. Mix the cornstarch mixture with the sauce in the pressure pot and stir well. Select Simmer on the settings, and bring the mixture to a boil while stirring constantly. Add fresh basil, and serve over rice.

If you are enjoying this book, I'd greatly appreciate it if you could leave a review. I'm always eager to listen to feedback so I can update and improve my books, and create new content!

25. Chicken Enchilada Pasta

Servings: 6

Ingredients

1 cup of diced onion

1 can (19 oz.) of enchilada sauce

1 ¼ cups of water

2 large skinless boneless chicken breasts, uncooked & diced

2 cups of shredded Mexican cheese

1 tablespoon of vegetable oil

2 cloves garlic, diced

1 (10 oz.) can of Rotel tomatoes

1.25 oz package of taco seasoning mix

3 cups of dried rotini pasta

Olives, Green onions, diced tomatoes, and cilantro to garnish

Directions

Heat oil in the pressure cooker pot, and then sauté the onion until tender, around five minutes. Stir in garlic and sauté for 1 more minute.

Mix in the taco seasoning, water, tomatoes, and enchilada sauce in the cooking pot. Add the pasta and diced chicken breasts.

Secure the lid, set the pressure to high, and then cook for four minutes. Turn the pressure cooker off, and apply a quick pressure release.

Select the "Sauté" setting, and cook while stirring for one minute, or until the pasta is tender.

Turn the pressure cooker of, and transfer the pasta into a baking dish (8x8). Top with the cheese, and broil until all the cheese has melted and is turning brown.

Serve topped with cilantro, diced tomatoes, olives, and green onions.

26. Almond Saffron Rice Pilaf

Servings: 6

Ingredients

1 ¼ cups of water

1 tablespoon of butter

1 celery stalk, finely chopped

½ teaspoon of salt

1 14 oz can of chicken broth

Pinch of saffron threads

1 medium onion, finely chopped

2 cups of long grain white rice, rinsed

½ cup of sliced almonds, toasted

Directions

Mix the water and broth in a small saucepan, and heat over medium heat. Stir the saffron into the liquid, and then remove from heat.

Melt butter in the cooking pressure pot, and then sauté the celery and chopped onions. Cook while stirring occasionally until tender, approximately three to five minutes.

Stir in the rice, and continue cooking while stirring frequently until opaque, approximately one to two minutes. Stir in the salt and saffron broth, and secure with the lid. Set the pressure to high, and select three minutes. When the beep sounds, leave it for five minutes before applying quick pressure release to get rid of the remaining pressure.

Remove the lid when the valve drops carefully, fluff the rice, and then stir in the almonds. Serve immediately

27. Minestrone Soup With Basil Pesto

Yields: 10 cups

Ingredients

1 large onion, finely chopped

3 carrots diced

2 14.5 ounce cans diced tomato

2 bay leaves

2 cups of digitali pasta, cooked

1 14.5 ounce cans kidney beans

3 - 4 tablespoons of basil pesto

1 tablespoon of olive oil

4 cloves garlic minced

1 cup of celery diced

5 cups of vegetable stock

1 teaspoon of salt

2 cups of baby spinach

½ teaspoon of freshly ground black pepper

Directions

Heat oil in the pressure cooker pot, select "Sauté", and cook the onion while stirring occasionally until tender, around five minutes. Mix in the celery, carrots, and garlic. Continue stirring and cooking for five more minutes.

Add the bay leaves, vegetable stock, tomatoes, and salt, and cover with the lid. Set the pressure to high, and cook for five minutes. When done, turn the pressure cooker off and give it five minutes before you apply a quick pressure release.

Remove the bay leaves, and stir in the beans, spinach, and pasta. Season with pepper, select "Keep Warm" in the cooker settings to keep the soup warm before serving, and then mix in the pesto when you are ready to serve.

28. French Dip Sandwiches

Servings: 2

Ingredients

1 can (14.5 oz.) of beef broth

1 teaspoon of dried rosemary

4 sub rolls, sliced lengthwise

1.5 lb boneless beef top round roast, sliced thinly

1 packet of dried onion soup mix

½ teaspoon of garlic powder

8 slices provolone cheese

Directions

Add rosemary, soup mix, garlic powder, and beef into the pressure cooker pot, and cover. Set the pressure to high, and select ten minutes cooking time. Wait for the beep, turn the cooker off, and apply a natural pressure release for ten minutes, followed with a quick pressure release to get rid of the remaining pressure.

Remove the meat, strain the broth, and skim out visible fat. Spread butter over the sub rolls, and toast under a broiler. Add 2 slices of cheese and meat at the top, and broil again until the cheese melts and starts bubbling. Serve with broth.

29. Grains And Kale Salad

Servings: 8-12

Ingredients

2 ½ cups of water

3 cups of packaged torn baby kale leaves

4 tablespoons of fresh lemon juice

1/3 cup of extra-virgin olive oil

¼ cup of crumbled feta

16 ounce package of Trader Joe's Harvest Grains Blend

1 teaspoon of salt

1/3 cup of finely diced red onion

Zest from one lemon

Salt & freshly ground pepper

Directions

Mix the harvest grains blend, salt, and water in the pressure cooker pot, and cover with the lid. Set the pressure to high and select three minutes cooking time. Once the beep sounds, turn off the pressure cooker, and apply a natural pressure release for ten minutes, followed with a quick pressure release. Transfer to a large bowl and leave to cool completely

Mix in the oil, lemon juice, lemon zest, onion, and kale, and season with salt & pepper. Sprinkle the feta over the top, and set aside for thirty minutes. Serve or store in the fridge for up to two days.

30. Pressure Cooker Smothered burritos

Servings: 6

Ingredients

16 oz. of enchilada sauce, divided

½ cup of water

2 cups of shredded cheese

3 lbs. cubed boneless beef rump roast

2 teaspoons beef base or 2 beef bouillon cubes

10 to12 burrito-size flour tortillas

Directions

Mix the bouillon, one cup of enchilada sauce, beef, and water in the cooking pot. Set the pressure to high, and select thirty minutes on the timer. Turn the pressure cooker off when the beep sounds, and apply a natural pressure release for ten minutes, followed by a quick pressure release. Remove the lid as soon as the valve drops.

Line a rimmed baking tray with aluminum foil and place a tortilla over. Add about half a cup of beef at the center, fold and roll into a burrito. Do the same with the other tortillas. Add shredded cheese and enchilada sauce at the top, and broil until the cheese melts and turns bubbly, approximately two to four minutes.

Side Dishes

31. Pressure Cooker Sun dried herbed tomato polenta

Servings: 6
Ingredients

½ cup of finely chopped onion

4 cups of vegetable stock or water

1 teaspoon of salt

2 teaspoons of fresh oregano-chopped, or ½ teaspoon dried

3 tablespoons of chopped fresh basil

1 cup of coarse polenta

1 - 2 tablespoons of olive oil, optional

2 teaspoons of minced garlic

1/3 cup of sun-dried tomatoes, finely diced

1 bay leaf

1 teaspoon of chopped fresh rosemary, or ¼ teaspoon dried

2 tablespoons of chopped fresh flat-leaf parsley

Directions

Heat oil in a pressure cooker pot, and then sauté the onion for one minute. Stir in the garlic and cook for one more minute.

Mix in the rosemary, oregano, bay leaf, salt, sun dried tomatoes, and water, as well as half of both the parsley and basil. Sprinkle with polenta over the top, but do not stir.

Secure with the lid, set the pressure to high, and cook for five minutes. Allow a natural pressure release for ten minutes, and then do a quick pressure release. Remove the lid, remove and get rid of the bay leaf. Stir the polenta and serve immediately.

32. Baked Beans

Servings: 10 to 12

Ingredients

8 cups of water

10-ounces of thick-sliced bacon, chopped into ½ inch pieces

2 ½ cups of water

½ cup of ketchup

1 teaspoon of dry mustard

¼ teaspoon of ground black pepper

1 pound of dried navy beans

1 tablespoon of salt

1 large onion, chopped

½ cup of molasses

¼ cup of packed brown sugar

½ teaspoon of salt

Directions

Rinse the beans in a colander, and remove any available debris. Dissolve one tablespoon of salt in eight cups of water in the pressure cooker pot, and soak the beans there. Drain & rinse the beans, and then get rid of the soaking liquid.

Set the cooker to "Browning" and toss in the bacon. Cook until crispy, approximately five minutes. Transfer the bacon onto a paper towel-lined plate. Cook the onion in the pot until tender, approximately three minutes.

Mix in the pepper, ½ teaspoon of salt, dry mustard, brown sugar, ketchup, molasses, and 2 ½ cups of water. Add the soaked beans and mix well.

Set the pressure to high, and select 35 minutes cooking time. Turn off the pressure cooker once the beeper rings, wait for ten minutes, and then apply a quick pressure release to get rid of the remaining pressure. Dispose off any floating beans, and check to see whether the beans are tender. If not, continue cooking for a few more minutes.

Mix in the cooked bacon, set the cooker to "Simmer", and cook the beans while stirring occasionally until the sauce achieves desired consistency.

33. Green Rice

Servings: 3

Ingredients

1 cup of uncooked long-grain rice

½ cup of fresh cilantro

Salt & freshly ground pepper, to taste

1 ¼ cups of low-sodium vegetable or chicken broth

Flesh ½ large ripe avocado

¼ cup of green salsa/green hot sauce

Directions

Mix the rice and broth in the pressure cooker pot, and secure with the lid. Set the pressure to high, and select three minutes cooking time. Turn the pressure cooker off when the beeper sounds, and apply a natural pressure release for ten minutes, followed by a quick pressure release to get rid of the remaining pressure.

Using a fork, fluff the rice and set it aside to cool. Mix together the salsa, cilantro, and avocado in a blender, and blend while adding a little water as required until it achieves a smooth consistency. Mix with the rice and season with salt & pepper.

34. Rosemary Garlic Potatoes

Servings: 2-4

Ingredients

1 tablespoon of olive oil

2 springs rosemary

1 pound of new potatoes, scrubbed & thinly sliced

2 garlic cloves, sliced

Directions

Insert a steamer basket into the pressure cooker pot, and then add the sliced potatoes and one cup of water. Secure with the lid, set the pressure to high and select four minutes cooking time.

Meanwhile, combine the rosemary, garlic, and oil in a small glass dish, and then slide into the microwave on high for one minute or until the garlic is fragrant.

Turn the pressure cooker off when the beep sounds, and apply a quick pressure release. Remove the steamer basket and potatoes carefully. Spread the potatoes over a rimmed baking sheet, and drizzle with the oil, garlic ad rosemary. Add salt and pepper to taste

35. Thai Quinoa Salad

Servings: 8

Ingredients

1 ½ cups of water

1 carrot, peeled & shredded

1 cup of frozen edamame, thawed

2 cups of shredded red cabbage

1 cup of quinoa, rinsed

½ teaspoon salt

1 cucumber, chopped

6 green onions, chopped

Dressing

¼ cup of lime juice

1 tablespoon of vegetable oil

1 tablespoon of sesame oil

½ cup of peanuts, chopped

2 tablespoons of chopped basil

1 tablespoon of soy sauce

2 tablespoons of sugar

1 tablespoon of freshly grated ginger

Pinch of red pepper flakes

¼ cup of freshly chopped cilantro

Directions

Combine the water, quinoa, and salt in the pressure cooking pot. Set the pressure to high, and select one minute cooking time. Once the beep sounds, turn off the pressure cooker, wait for ten minutes, and then apply a quick pressure release to get rid of any remaining pressure. Lift out of the pot and set aside to cool.

Add the vegetables and cooled quinoa in a large bowl. In a separate smaller bowl, mix together the red pepper flakes, sesame oil, vegetable oil, sugar, lime juice, and soy sauce until all the sugar has dissolved. Add more red pepper flakes or sugar to taste, if needed. Top the quinoa & vegetables with the dressing, and stir to mix. Spread the peanuts, basil, and cilantro over the salad, and mix lightly. Serve or store in the fridge for up to one day.

36. Pork Sirloin Tip roast

Servings: 6 - 8

Ingredients

½ teaspoon of salt

½ teaspoon of garlic powder

3 pound pork sirloin tip roast

1 cup of water

½ teaspoon of coarse black pepper

½ teaspoon of onion powder

¼ teaspoon of chili powder

1 tablespoon of vegetable oil

½ cup of apple juice

Directions

Combine the spices in a small bowl and mix. Rub the mixture around the pork roast.

Select "Browning" in the pressure cooker, and heat the oil in the cooking pot. Brown the pork roast on either side, and then add the apple juice and water.

Secure the lid, and set the pressure to high. Cook for twenty five minutes, and then apply a natural pressure release for five minutes. Do a quick pressure release to get rid of the remaining pressure, and then remove the lid. Serve immediately.

37. Pressure Cooker Black Bean Rice Salad

Servings: 4-8

Ingredients

1 ½ cups of water

1 (14 oz.) can of black beans, drained & rinsed

1 avocado, diced

1 cup of brown rice

¼ teaspoon of salt

12 grape tomatoes, quartered

¼ cup of minced cilantro

Spicy Dressing:

2 teaspoons of Cholula or Tabasco

1 teaspoon of agave nectar

3 tablespoons of extra-virgin olive oil

3 tablespoons of fresh lime juice

2 garlic cloves, minced or pressed

1/8 teaspoon of salt

Directions

Mix the rice, salt, and water in the pressure cooker pot, and cover with the lid. Set the pressure to high, and select twenty four minutes cooking time. Turn the pressure cooker off once the beep sounds, and apply a natural pressure release for ten minutes. Do a quick pressure release to get rid of any remaining pressure. Remove the lid carefully when the valve drops.

In a large bowl, mix together the cilantro, avocado, tomato, black beans, and brown rice. Spread the dressing over, and mix.

The dressing

Whisk together the agave, garlic, salt, Tabasco, and lime juice in a small bowl, and add the olive oil.

38. Pressure Cooker Black Beans

Servings: 2

Ingredients

2/3 cup of water

1 sprig epazote (optional)

½ teaspoon of cumin seeds

1 cup of black beans, quick soaked or soaked overnight

1 piece of kombu seaweed

1-2 cloves garlic

Salt to taste

Directions

Mix the spices, herb, garlic, kombu, beans, and water in the pressure cooker. Select high pressure and high heat, and cook for five minutes. After the five minutes, allow the pressure to drop naturally, and test if the beans are cooked. If not, cook them for one or two more minutes in the pressure cooker.

Remove the lid, and remove the epazote and kombu. Add salt to taste.

Conclusion

Thank you again for downloading this book!

I hope this book was able to help you to know various recipes you can prepare using your pressure cooker.

The next step is to start preparing some of these meals so that you can know how best to use your pressure cooker.